METAL SPINNING

Reagan & Smith

Lindsay Publications Inc.

A Metal Spinner at Work.

METAL SPINNING

For Craftsmen, Instructors, and Students

JAMES E. REAGAN

and

EARL E. SMITH

*Instructors of Metalwork, John Adams High School,
Cleveland, Ohio*

Metal Spinning

by James E. Reagan and Earl E. Smith

Original copyright 1936
by Bruce Publishing, New York

Reprinted by
Lindsay Publications Inc
Bradley IL 60915

ISBN 0-917914-83-X

1991

9   10   11   12   13

WARNING

INTRODUCTION

Metal spinning was suggested as a manual-training subject quite early in the history of industrial arts, but because of difficulties of organization and technique, and an almost complete lack of information concerning the work, it failed to establish itself as one of the traditional industrial-arts activities.

With the organization of the junior high school and the rather common acceptance of the principle of the general shop, conditions more favorable to the success of metal spinning have developed, and recently there has been a revival of interest in this type of metalwork, with promise of its finding an important place as a unit in the general metalwork course of study.

The task of developing metal spinning as an educational subject was assumed by the authors of this little book. Skilled as metalworkers, experienced as teachers, and professionally equipped for the task, they have selected and placed in educational form those elements of the trade adapted to the educational needs and capabilities of pupils of the upper junior-high-school and senior-high-school grades. They have also chosen and designed the necessary simple equipment for doing the work. Their work has been developed under most favorable classroom conditions, and every project presented has been successfully executed by pupils under their instruction.

Primarily the work developed here is educational rather than vocational. Metal spinning is an intensely interesting subject, demanding skill and judgment; it gives contacts with a variety of metals not commonly used in industrial-arts work; it provides splendid opportunity for art expression in line and form. The art possibilities of the work are evidenced by the type of projects presented in the book.

The authors are to be congratulated upon their contribution to the cause of educational handwork.

WILLIAM E. ROBERTS,
Supervisor of Manual Arts,
Cleveland, Ohio

WARNING

Remember that the materials and methods described here are from another era. Workers were less safety conscious then, and some methods may be downright dangerous. Be careful! Use good solid judgement in your work, and think ahead. Lindsay Publications Inc. has not tested these methods and materials and does not endorse them. Our job is merely to pass along to you information from another era. Safety is your responsibility.

Write for a complete catalog of unusual books available from:

Lindsay Publications Inc
PO Box 12
Bradley IL 60915-0012

PREFACE

This book has been written in response to a great number of requests which have been received by us from industrial-arts instructors and craftsmen who wish to know more about metal spinning.

The metal spinners of the past thought, like many other old masters, that their art should be taught only by example and imitation, and that the introduction of printed information about it would cause endless confusion. This idea has limited the knowledge of metal spinning to a very few people and has made it almost impossible to get any adequate information on the subject.

We have tried, in this book, to meet the needs of students who have had little or no experience in this subject, as well as to be of assistance to the craftsman, who is already doing a limited amount of metal spinning. We have endeavored to present the work in a simple step-by-step manner so the reader will be able to proceed with full assurance that it will be possible for him to do the work he has undertaken.

It contains specific information as to the mechanical set-up for metal spinning, using ordinary lathes which may be found in home and school shops.

This book will also be very valuable for use in industrial-arts courses in teacher-training schools 'where it is desirable to establish practical branches of metalwork that will attract students and receive favorable comment from industry.

We have added an appendix to this book for teachers, who wish to add metal spinning to their metal-shop units. We hope it will contribute to their efficiency in this subject and add to their enjoyment in teaching it. If it does, our aim has been accomplished.

Much genuine pleasure has been derived from the writing of this book, and we hope we have conveyed to our readers the enthusiasm we have for this branch of metalwork.

We send it forth in the hope that it will prove an aid and encouragement to those who desire to know more about metal spinning.

This book is based on actual results, obtained in a school metal shop where the authors of the book are the shop instructors.

EARL E. SMITH
JAMES E. REAGAN

CONTENTS

Chapter I

HISTORICAL FACTS ABOUT METAL SPINNING

Metal spinning is a craft that may well be called an art. It is the shaping of a revolving disk of metal on a lathe over a wooden or metal form called a chuck, by means of pressure applied with a spinning tool. In these days when we hear so much of speed and efficiency this painstaking art has been losing ground.

It is a very rare instance when an American boy takes up spinning as his lifework. Most of the spinners who work at this craft in America are men who learned their trade in Europe. In some cases, of course, we hear of a father who had handed down his trade to his son. In the United States at the present time the artisans who do metal spinning are recognized as skillful craftsmen and their wages are unusually high.

Metal spinning is one of the older crafts. This trade was first developed by a small group of artisans in Europe, particularly in France, Germany, and Sweden. They jealously guarded their trade, formed their own trade guilds, and set up a seven years' apprenticeship for spinners. The boys started their apprenticeship at the age of fourteen or fifteen and were required to serve a year at observing before they were allowed to use any of the spinning tools.

Metal spinning was first introduced in the United States about 1840 by a man named Jordan. He started a small shop in New York City and tried to enlarge his business by teaching it to several apprentices. After they became experienced enough in that art, they started in business for themselves. Some of these boys stayed in business until they were old men. Most of them became specialists in some line of the work. Some of the best and most expert sterling-silver spinners learned their trade in these shops.

Oval spinning was introduced in the United States about 1865 by the P. Prybil Machine Company. They make a specialty of making lathes and oval chucks.

In the United States the metal-spinning industry is centered in the larger cities. Chicago is probably the largest center, while Philadelphia, New York, Cleveland, and Boston do a proportionate share of the work.

Other places have shops where spinning is done but these usually have it as a side line to their real business.

Though metal spinning has been replaced to a great extent by pressing and stamping, they can never take its place entirely, as there are many cases when the form to be produced cannot be made in one piece except by spinning. If stamped or pressed they would have to be produced in parts and then soldered or riveted together. This, of course, is not desirable in many cases from either a standpoint of art or of strength.

Also for economical reasons stamping or pressing cannot replace spinning, as the stamping and pressing equipment is so costly that unless at least 100,000 pieces are to be produced, it is far cheaper to spin the articles desired.

Metal spinning is not a new idea in schools, for as far back as 1898 the working of aluminum was introduced into India in the Madras School of Arts. The bulk of the work was done by the spinning process. But it is new in the schools of the United States. Very little has been done in this line of metalwork, partly due to lack of informational material. But now that this obstacle can be overcome it is hoped that this craft or art, whichever you may choose to call it, will gain a new foothold and become a popular activity among the students and craftsmen of this country.

Example of Early American
Spinning.

Chapter II

INTEREST APPEAL OF METAL SPINNING

Metal spinning has from its origin been kept in the hands of a few craftsmen, who have guarded the secrets of their trade so well, that to most people there seems to be something very difficult and mysterious about this art.

The idea of doing something mysterious and new appeals to both young and old. The beginner, when once introduced to this work, soon becomes so fascinated and interested, that he quickly becomes an enthusiastic student of the art of metal spinning.

The opportunity for finding spinning projects is almost unlimited. In fact, the majority of the articles offered in our stores, as products of metal spinning, can very easily be reproduced by the student after a little practice. Cooking utensils like pie pans, cake pans, and saucepans have all proved to be successful spinning projects. A camping outfit, consisting of a skillet, a kettle with a lid, a dish and a cup, appeals to boys and men who enjoy hiking and camping trips. One who takes pride in his outdoor cookery gets an added satisfaction in using cooking utensils of his own manufacture.

We have found in our experience that most beginners prefer to make the more artistic articles, like lamps, candlesticks, ash trays, and comports. These have been made of pewter, copper, or brass and the work is of such a high grade that it is impossible to distinguish them from similar articles that are sold in our most exclusive stores.

The student of metalwork has always been confronted by the difficulty of finding metalworking projects, for which the materials cost less than does the finished article when sold at retail. This is not the case in metal spinning where the retail price is many times the cost of the metal used, in some cases as much as one hundred per cent more. The home craftsman may, if he desires, use discarded sheet-metal utensils to secure material for metal spinning. Anything from copper wash boilers to copper stills have been spun into beautiful copper lamps, while discarded aluminum household utensils have been changed into camping outfits.

Metal spinning offers an opportunity to produce articles of real artistic value. Craftsmen, who know how much criticism is given to inartistic projects, will appreciate that they can learn readily how to spin articles of excellent design which possess the perfection in workmanship found in similar commercial articles.

A Spinner Spinning.

The beginner in metal spinning soon comes to have the feeling of satisfaction experienced by those who have produced a piece of superior workmanship. He also realizes that the work he is doing compares very favorably with the work turned out by industry. He may not turn out as much work as an experienced spinner does, but his work will be just as good.

The person who takes up metal spinning as a home activity or hobby may find that it leads directly to a position in industry for him. Recently new fields have opened for the metal spinner. One of these is the electrical field in the building industry. All ornamental chandelier work is spun, as new designs are constantly in demand and there are so few of each kind made that it would not pay to go to the expense of stamping them.

Another field is the airplane industry. Airplanes are not made in sufficient quantities to warrant the expense of making dies for the various shells that are used, so the metal spinner is called upon to do this work.

No one of average mechanical knowledge and ability should hesitate to make a set-up for metal spinning. He need not hesitate from the standpoint of expense for if there is a lathe available the cost is nominal. The authors know of one successful installation where the cash outlay was only fifty cents.

A person attempting metal spinning must give thought and study to the work, and must be willing to spend time in experimenting, but when he produces his first perfect article he will experience a feeling of joy and satisfaction that will amply repay him for the time and energy he has spent.

Copper Lamp.

Chapter III

THE MECHANICAL SET-UP FOR METAL SPINNING

Metal spinning requires suitable equipment to do satisfactory work, and this chapter contains clear and concise directions so that the spinner may properly equip his spinning unit. There are few machine-tool companies that make special lathes for metal spinning and most commercial companies transform lathes built for other purposes into spinning lathes. Hence, the school or the home worker will have to follow suit and make his own mechanical set-up. Fortunately this may be done with a very

Engine Lathe Set Up for Spinning.

small outlay of money. The spinning lathe may be made over from an engine lathe, or from a heavy-duty wood lathe equipped with variable-speed motor head. The lathe should be of sturdy construction and equipped for variable speeds. Speeds should range from 300 up by at least four steps. Until recently top speeds were around 1900 r.p.m. A good spinner can do perfect work at 300 r.p.m., and 1500 to 1800 top speed is sufficient for a school shop. Of course an increase in speed gives increased production. Modern spinners work at speeds from 2500 to 3000. These speeds should only be attempted by the skilled spinner. The equipment of the lathe for metal spinning differs from the corresponding equipment for a lathe used for metal turning in regard to the headstock, faceplate, toolrest, and tail center. The ordinary faceplate may be used to hold the chucks in metal spinning. However, a much more desirable set-up may be made by boring out the base of the wood forms used to make the wooden chucks and cutting screw threads in them corresponding in size and pitch to those of the lathe spindle and then screwing this threaded chuck directly on the lathe spindle, thus eliminating entirely the use of faceplates. Further information in regard to making these threaded chucks will be given in the chapter on "Chucks for Metal Spinning."

Due to the heavy end thrust on the spindle bearings during metal spinning, it is advisable to either secure a lathe equipped with thrust bearings on the spindle shaft, or to so equip the lathe selected for a spinning lathe. This is, of course, more necessary for continuous heavy-duty work in industry than in a school shop. The writers have seen a very high quality of work done in school metal shops on ordinary engine lathes which were not equipped with thrust bearings and which stood up under constant service for a considerable length of time without noticeable wear on the spindle bearings.

The screw-spindle and handwheel tailstock as usually found on engine lathes and wood-turning lathes is perfectly satisfactory for metal spinning. Lathes which have been transformed into spinning lathes by industry use this type of tailstock for heavy work and on shallow shells. However, for deep shells and on shells made of light-gauge metal, many commercial spinning lathes are equipped with a sliding spindle and cam lever for quick adjustment of the tailstock. This permits of quick insertion of the disks of metal to be spun and the quick removal of the finished shell which greatly increases the production on the lathe. This feature is, of course, not necessary in the school or home shop.

After the proper lathe for transformation has been selected, the bearings on the spindle must be checked for strength to stand end thrust, and the requirements of variable speeds of the proper r.p.m. must be made. The next thing to consider, then, is the making of the toolrest or spinning rest, which is a very important part of the spinning-lathe set-up. It is of simple design, and may be made easily from the stock usually found in metal shops. Its basic principle is the same as that of the rest on the wood lathe except that vertical holes are bored in it at intervals

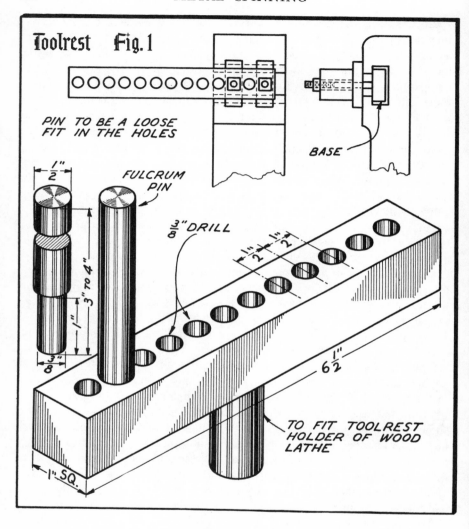

Toolrest   Fig. 1

PIN TO BE A LOOSE
FIT IN THE HOLES

BASE

FULCRUM
PIN

$\frac{3}{8}$" DRILL

$\frac{1}{2}$"

$\frac{1}{2}$" $\frac{1}{2}$"

3" TO 4"

1"

$\frac{3}{8}$"

6$\frac{1}{2}$"

TO FIT TOOLREST
HOLDER OF WOOD
LATHE

1" SQ.

of ½ in. for the purpose of inserting a steel pin which acts as a fulcrum
for the spinning tool. This fulcrum pin is shouldered so that it will not
drop through the hole and must be a free fit so that it may be easily
moved from hole to hole as the spinning progresses toward the head of
the lathe. One-inch square stock should be used for the horizontal portion
of the rest. Three-eighths-inch holes should be bored in it vertically at
½-in. intervals for its entire length.

The base of the toolrest should be machined to correspond to the slot in the compound rest of the lathe if an engine lathe is used. The base should be firmly bolted to the horizontal piece with two bolts ⅜ in. in diameter and a third piece should be bolted between the two sufficient in height to bring the top of the horizontal piece or rest level with the center of the spindle shaft. If the toolrest is cast of steel, it can be made of one piece. The base should be designed to fit either the compound rest of an engine lathe, or the rest holder of a wood lathe as the case may be. In either case allow sufficient metal so that it may be machined to size. Figure 1 shows the set-up for both an engine lathe and a wood lathe.

The fulcrum pin shown in Figure 1 should be a free fit in the holes of the toolrest. Some craftsmen prefer a tapered pin to fit into tapered holes. This gives, of course, absolute rigidity of the fulcrum which is desirable. But it has the disadvantage of easily becoming locked in the hole.

When the wear on the straight pin becomes excessive after long use, causing a rocking motion to the fulcrum pin, it should be replaced with a new one. At least one year's hard service can be expected before this is necessary. When an engine lathe is used, the operator may prefer to shift his lathe carriage from time to time in place of shifting the fulcrum pin in order to keep his spinning tool at right angles to the point of contact with the spinning chuck. However, it will be necessary to shift the fulcrum pin occasionally for most efficient work.

The spinning center is probably the most important part of the mechanical set-up necessary in transforming any lathe for metal spinning. This vital part of the spinning lathe has passed through several stages of evolution from a very crude spinning center which was not durable and needed replacing frequently to a perfected spinning center which is very dependable and may be used for an indefinite period of time in metal spinning. Three stages in the evolution of spinning centers are illustrated by Figures 2, 3, and 4.

The one shown in Figure 2 is made by machining a piece of steel or phosphor bronze to the dimensions shown. A steel ball is inserted in the hole so that the friction unit may stand the end thrust and still run free. The unit is assembled with grease. This type of center, while much more preferable to the type shown in Figure 3, still has its drawbacks in regard to durability.

The spinning center shown in Figure 3 is simply a piece of steel machined to the size and taper shown. A hole is bored into the opposite end, and a block of wood or fiber turned to run freely in it. This block is the friction unit of the spinning center. The lubrication used is grease. There should be at least .001 in. clearance between the moving parts so that the grease may prevent heating while the spinning center is working under pressure.

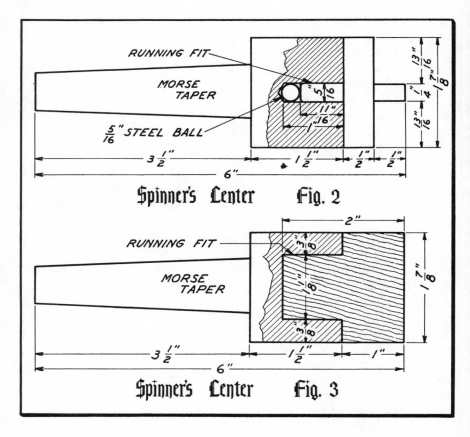

The spinning center shown in Figure 4 was designed by the authors and has been found most satisfactory in use. Any person who is transforming a lathe for metal spinning is urged to take the time required to make such a spinning center, as it assists greatly in doing satisfactory work. Many attempts at this type of work have failed, because the spinning centers used were crudely made.

In making the spinning center shown in Figure 4, a lathe center

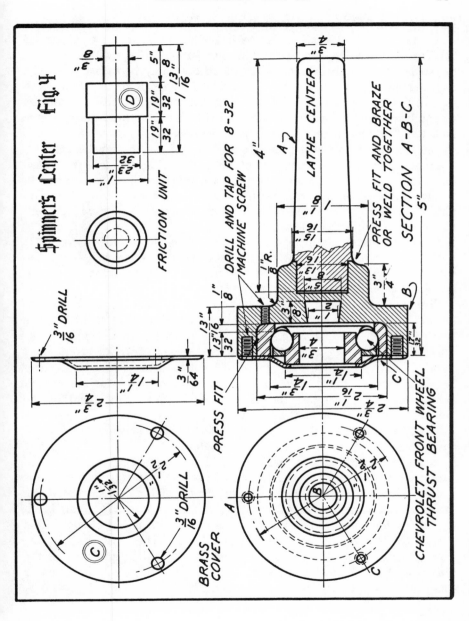

Spinners Center Fig. 4

FRICTION UNIT

$\frac{3}{8}$"

5"

8

$\frac{13}{16}$"

$\frac{19}{32}$ $\frac{19}{32}$

D

$\frac{23}{32}$

1"

$\frac{3}{16}$" DRILL

$2\frac{3}{4}$"

$1\frac{1}{4}$"

$\frac{3}{64}$"

PRESS FIT

BRASS COVER

$\frac{3}{16}$" DRILL

2"

$1\frac{13}{16}$"

C

A

LATHE CENTER

PRESS FIT AND BRAZE OR WELD TOGETHER

SECTION A-B-C

DRILL AND TAP FOR 8-32 MACHINE SCREW

4"

$\frac{3}{4}$"

$1\frac{1}{8}$"

$1\frac{15}{16}$"

$\frac{1}{8}$" R.

$1\frac{13}{16}$"

$1\frac{3}{8}$"

$\frac{5}{8}$"

$\frac{3}{4}$"

B

$\frac{1}{8}$"

$\frac{13}{32}$" 6

$\frac{3}{8}$"

$1\frac{1}{2}$"

$\frac{3}{4}$"

$1\frac{1}{4}$"

$2\frac{3}{16}$"

$2\frac{3}{4}$"

$\frac{17}{32}$"

C

5"

CHEVROLET FRONT WHEEL THRUST BEARING

2"

may be used for shank A. Part B may be made of either steel or cast iron, first turning the recess for the insertion of the center to a pressed fit. The next step is to press part A into part B. The two should then be welded or brazed together, after which they may be turned as a unit by inserting them in the lathe spindle. Turn part B to the dimensions shown, paying particular attention that the recess for the race of the thrust bearing is a pressed fit. Next drill and tap three holes in the face B for 8/32 machine screws, to hold brass cover C.

Before the race is pressed into place, drill and tap three holes for 8/32 machine screws. These holes cannot be drilled after the race is pressed into place. The holes are for the purpose of inserting a drift punch to remove the race in case the bearing should ever break down. They are tapped out for the insertion of 8/32 machine screws, which will prevent the lubricant from flowing out.

The cover plate C is made from a piece of 18- or 20-gauge brass.

Next, the cone of the bearing, the race and recess are well lubricated with a heavy grease, preferably automobile universal-joint or wheel-bearing grease, and then assembled.

Then the brass cover C should be fastened in place with 8/32 round-headed machine screws to retain the cone and lubricant in place. The bearing used in the spinning center made by the authors was a front-wheel thrust bearing from the outer end of a Chevrolet front-wheel spindle. Any thrust bearing of similar dimensions, of course, may be used, making the proper changes in dimension for its insertion in part B and also changing the center hole in C to correspond to the dimensions of the cone of the bearing.

Next, the friction unit D should be made. This unit should be turned out of cold-rolled steel to the dimensions shown. This friction unit while it rotates in spinning is in reality a dead unit and does not need to be hardened for service. The friction unit D is used for all types of shells which permit boring a $\frac{3}{8}$-in. hole in the center of the disk. For spinning shells such as pans, trays, or bowls, it is necessary to add a tail block to the friction unit D. The tail block is made with a $\frac{3}{8}$-in. hole drilled sufficiently deep to slip over the $\frac{3}{8}$ end of section D so that the spinning may be accomplished without the necessity of drilling any hole in the center of the disk. Detailed description of tail blocks will be given in Chapter V on "Chucks for Metal Spinning."

Chapter IV

SPINNING TOOLS

The spinner's trade is one of the few trades in which the hand tools used in his craft are not standardized as to size and dimensions. Every spinner makes his own tools to correspond to the individual requirements of the work he is doing and also varies them to suit his own personal ideas in their manufacture. However, the spinner's hand tools can be separated into three general classes: blunt tools, beading tools, and tools with cutting edges. The blunt tools are the most numerous in shapes and kinds. A beading-wheel holder with a number of different size wheels make up the second group. One or two tools with cutting edges fill the requirements for most work. Every spinner in industry has a large collection of hand tools which vary greatly as to shape and size. Few spinning jobs may be completed by using any one tool. However, there are several tools of standard shape which have been developed by the old-time craftsmen. Many tools are made, however, which vary greatly from the standard shapes for use in different classes of metal spinning and for different types of metal.

The tools of standard shape which are the only ones necessary for a person outfitting a shop are the round nose, diamond point, tongue, beading, and planisher. These are shown in Figure 5.

All of these tools except the diamond-point tool are used with the end of the tool placed beneath the center of the work. One who is taking up metal spinning for the first time should practice laying the spinning tool on the metal disk and manipulating it below the center of the work. He should be careful not to force or push the tool straight into a spinning disk until he is thoroughly proficient in his work. This will avoid injury to the beginner.

All spinning tools with the exception noted before are used by forcing the end of the tool against the spinning disk. As a result friction ensues. To reduce this friction as much as possible, the end of the tool should be finished to a glasslike smoothness and hardened at the extreme end, leaving the rest of the shaft tough so that it is not so liable to break or snap off while in use. After the hardening process has been ac-

23

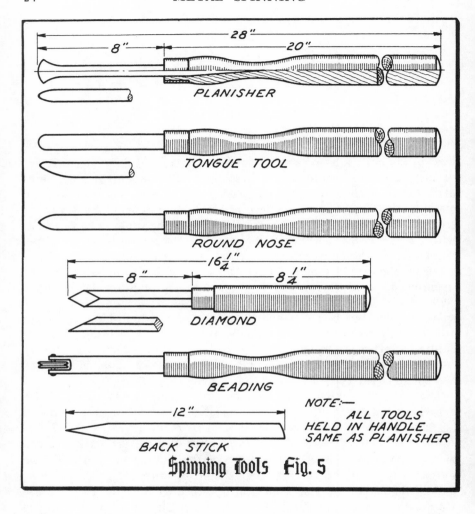

PLANISHER

TONGUE TOOL

ROUND NOSE

DIAMOND

BEADING

BACK STICK

NOTE:—
ALL TOOLS
HELD IN HANDLE
SAME AS PLANISHER

𝕾pinning 𝕿ools   𝕱ig. 5

complished, the end of the tool should again be polished to a mirrorlike finish. The large size of spinning tools is usually a surprise to a person unfamiliar with spinning. This size is necessary because of the great pressure and leverage which must be exerted in the spinning process.

An average size tool for metal spinning requires a piece of tool steel ½ to ¾ in. in diameter, and 18 in. long. This is inserted in an ash or hickory handle, which is the size of a baseball bat 1½ in. in diameter and 20 to 24 in. long, making the combined length of the tool at least

30 in. In fact, baseball bats have been used by spinners to form the handles of their tools. If this is to be done, the handle end of the baseball bat must be cut off, leaving the bat approximately 24 in. long. A ferrule, made from a section of iron or brass pipe, is then forced over the end, after which the end of the spinning tool, which is forged to a square point, is inserted in the handle.

The tongue tool should be made of tool steel since extreme hardening of the point is necessary. The diameter of the tongue tool may vary from $\frac{1}{2}$ to $\frac{3}{4}$ in. Round stock is always considered best; however, hexagonal stock may be used. About 4 in. of the end of the tool is ground and filed to shape after which it is polished and hardened, care being exercised to see that the extreme tip is never sharp, for that might tear the revolving metal.

The flat side of the tool should have its corners rounded and the extreme tip blunt so that the metal will not be torn during the spinning process.

Many craftsmen use this tool more than any other in their spinning, and in almost every case it is the tool used in preference to all other tools in the breaking down of a disk when beginning to spin. There has been no other tool as yet made which surpasses this tool in compressing the metal when smoothing out irregularities and wrinkles before removing the metal from the chuck.

The round-nose tool is a forming tool for small projects. Its shape is shown in Figure 5. It is also used as a finishing tool for small radii and for squaring up corners.

It may be made of $\frac{3}{4}$-in. round or hexagonal tool steel by grinding and filing to shape, taking care to see that the end is ground without burning. The end should be shaped to a blunt point and should be hardened and polished to a glasslike finish. This is a very efficient tool, and in many cases is used in preference to the tongue tool especially in the final stages of spinning.

The planishing tool or planisher is the third tool in importance. It is forged from $\frac{5}{8}$- to $\frac{3}{4}$-in. round tool steel to conform to the shape shown in Figure 5. It is quite necessary that the tool should be ground and polished accurately, using especial care to have the two flat, tapering surfaces true and smooth. After the tool has been forged, ground, and hardened, it should be polished to a glasslike finish. It is used as a finishing tool to remove tool marks left by the round-nose and other tools. The edge of the tool at its end may be used to make more perfect small grooves, coves, or shoulders in the shell.

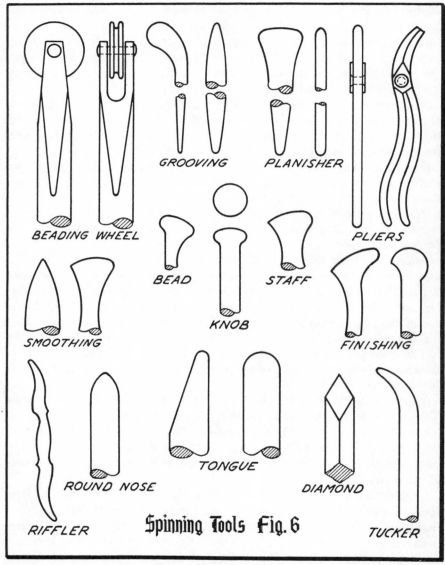

GROOVING

PLANISHER

BEADING WHEEL

PLIERS

BEAD

STAFF

KNOB

SMOOTHING

FINISHING

ROUND NOSE

TONGUE

DIAMOND

RIFFLER

Spinning Tools Fig. 6

TUCKER

The diamond-point tool is made from a ½-in. square piece of self-hardening tool steel and is ground to conform to the usual diamond-point shape used for metal cutting. This tool is used for trimming the edge of the metal disk to the exact size necessary previous to laying down the last quarter inch of metal on the chuck.

The beading tool is made as shown in Figure 5. It is used to turn a bead when necessary. The beading wheel may vary in diameter from 1 to 2 in., and the concave section of the face of the wheel varies in depth and width according to the size of the bead which is desired.

The foregoing tools are the only ones necessary to do the usual type of metal spinning which will be attempted by the beginner. Other tools shown in Figure 6 may be made by any person who is attempting unusually difficult spinning.

Each tool can be varied slightly to suit personal preference or the job being spun. It would be desirable to have each tool made in a different size varying by $\frac{1}{8}$ of an inch in diameter. This is a matter of personal preference, although some commercial spinners feel that they need a dozen or two of different spinning tools in order to do satisfactory work, while other spinners who can produce just as craftsmanlike work use but four or five tools.

It must be remembered that the foregoing tools, with the exception of the diamond-point tool, are for spinning metal of all kinds except steel. For spinning steel, brass or phosphor-bronze tools must be used. They should be made identical in shape with the ones just described. The spinning of steel is not recommended for the school shop except in articles of very shallow depth.

Tools made of hickory may be used as breaking-down tools for copper and pewter.

The backstick, Figure 5, is a piece of hard wood, 12 or 14 in. long. It is ground or shaped to a chisel point similar to that of a blunt cold chisel, and its use is described in the chapter on "The Technique of the Metal-Spinning Process." A very satisfactory backstick may be made from a hammer handle or from a broomstick. The length should be from 12 to 14 in.

A skimmer tool may be made from the same stock used for the diamond-point tool ground to the shape shown by the dotted lines.

Other tools such as the knob-nose tool, staff tool, grooving tool, and riffler are shown in Figure 6. They may be made as necessity requires.

Spinner's tools should be cared for as carefully as any other high-grade tools. They should be kept oiled when not in use in order that rust does not attack the polished surfaces as this would seriously impair their efficiency.

The smoother, brighter, and more glasslike the tools can be kept the easier it is to produce articles of a high standard of workmanship with them.

A very good way to care for spinning tools is to fasten a piece of heavy sole leather about 8 or 10 in. on a strip of hard wood with the hair side down, and on this sprinkle some putty powder. Rubbing the points of the tools on this hone will keep them always with a glasslike polish. Before polishing the tools in this manner, all oil should be removed from the end of the tool. The tool will groove itself into the leather which aids in the polishing process.

Handles for the spinner's tools may be made of hickory or ash $1\frac{1}{2}$ in. in diameter, 20 to 24 in. long, well ferruled at the end and turned on a wood lathe to approximately the shape of a wood-lathe tool handle.

Example of Early American
Spinning.

Chapter V

CHUCKS FOR METAL SPINNING

The wooden or metal form over which the shell of metal is spun is called a chuck. Every article that is to be spun must have its own chuck. For ordinary work the wooden chuck is used more frequently than the metal chuck. In selecting material for a wooden chuck, it is very important to find a wood that will stand up under pressure. A soft wood will not do this. Also the wood must have a close grain, as a coarse grain will

Group of Wooden Chucks.

splinter out after it has been used a few times. Maple is probably the most satisfactory and makes an almost ideal chuck; however, birch and lignum vitae are also suitable, although birch has a tendency to compress with the grain and has to be trued up frequently. Lignum vitae is very expensive, hence it is not used as often as the other woods.

In addition to wooden chucks, chucks made of wood covered with metal, of cast iron, and of steel are used.

Metal chucks are used only when there are a large number of shells to be spun. Steel chucks are used when there are corners and recesses to be spun, because it is necessary for the sharp corners to stand up under the constant use.

In making a cast-iron chuck, the pattern must be made large enough to permit of the removal of enough stock on the engine lathe to smooth up the chuck.

For most of the work in metal spinning done by the student, wooden chucks are advisable, hence the making of these will be described here. Any person who is able to turn out a well-balanced and artistic piece of wood turning, will be able to turn up the forms or chucks for the articles that are to be spun.

Wooden chucks screwed to faceplates are used in a few schools and colleges, where metal spinning is done. This plan requires a large number of faceplates, as the chucks cannot be removed from them until they are to be discarded. It is better to copy the method used in industry in the making of chucks, and cut threads directly in the base of the chuck so that it screws on the lathe spindle. This eliminates the use of the faceplate in spinning.

In making chucks, 2-in. maple blanks are cut to a circular form on the band saw approximately ½ in. larger than the diameter necessary for the finished chuck. Before gluing the blanks together, the blank which is to form the base of the chuck is chucked in the lathe and a hole bored

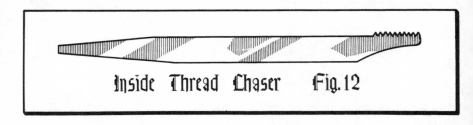

Inside Thread Chaser   Fig. 12

through it 3/16 in. smaller in diameter than the lathe spindle. It is necessary that this hole be bored and the threads cut before the form is glued up, because it is much easier to hold in the lathe chuck than after gluing up the entire chuck. Next a thread chaser, Figure 12, with the same number of threads to the inch as that of the lathe spindle is used to cut internal threads in the 2-in. maple blank. This may be done by using the tool holder of the lathe as a toolrest and operating the thread chaser in a manner similar to that of using a round-nosed lathe tool for boring wood turning. The person who has never used a thread chaser for cutting internal threads in wood, will be apt to have a feeling they cannot be cut in this manner as only boring action will result. But the authors have demonstrated to their own satisfaction that only a little experience is needed to cut perfect threads. Of course it is necessary to remove the chuck occasionally and test the size of the threaded bore by screwing it on the spindle of the spinning lathe. A number of these wooden blanks may be made up and threaded to fit the lathe spindle and kept in stock. Then the making of wooden chucks is simply a matter of gluing on the

Thread Chaser in Use.

additional stock necessary for turning to size. After the wooden forms for the chucks have been glued up and allowed to dry thoroughly, they are turned onto the lathe spindle of the spinning lathe. This is to make sure that the finished chuck runs true. A template may be used to insure accuracy.

When the chuck is completed it must be smoothed with sandpaper and a ⅜-in. hole bored in the center 1¼ in. deep. This hole is for the insertion of the ⅜-in. extension of the friction unit. A cross section of an ordinary chuck is shown in Figure 7.

A chuck must stand considerable abuse, and it is sometimes doubtful as to whether it will hold out for the job. If a number of similar shells are to be spun and the chuck shows signs of wear before all the shells desired have been finished, it is often possible to salvage the chuck by truing it up and spinning a metal shell over it. A groove is cut in the chuck ⅛ in. deep and ⅛ in. wide approximately ¼ in. above the height reached by the shells being spun. Next, a metal shell is spun over the wooden form until the groove has been reached. Then this shell is removed and annealed and then spun perfectly tight to the chuck. Finally the edge is trimmed and turned down into the groove provided for it. This type of chuck stands up very well for general use.

Cast iron makes a chuck that will last a great deal longer than wood and will produce very uniform shells. Cast-iron chucks should be made with just enough finish to produce the desired shape, as the removing

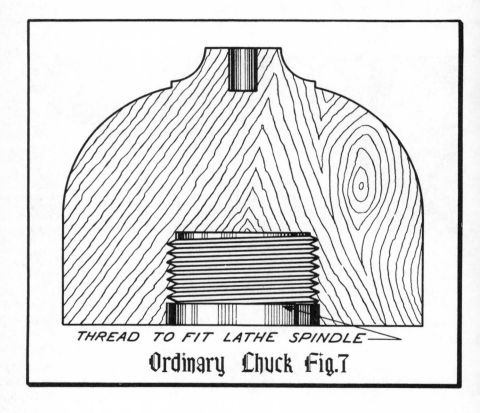

THREAD TO FIT LATHE SPINDLE

Ordinary Chuck Fig.7

of too much metal might expose sand holes in the casting and so make it unfit for a spinning form.

The chuck should be finished on the lathe where the spinning is to be done, as a chuck running out of a true is not only a poor tool but a dangerous one as well.

Cast-iron chucks are much easier made than steel ones but they are brittle and the corners and projections will chip off. Cold-rolled steel stands up under use and wears indefinitely.

Sometimes when a job calls for a slender or vaselike shape, it is desirable to use what the spinner calls "breaking-down" chucks. The metal is spun over each of these in turn until the desired shape has been secured

Metal-Covered Chucks.

for the final spinning over the true chuck. After each of these preliminary chucks have been used, the metal must be annealed. As many as four of these chucks may be used in the making of some deep, slim projects. These breaking-down chucks are to prevent the metal from weakening and so becoming too thin for successful spinning.

Besides the solid chucks described so far, there are sectional or knock-down chucks required by certain kinds of projects. These chucks may be described as being built in three sections; namely, an arbor, segments,

Cast-Iron Chucks for Lamp.

and a cover plate. The arbor must be slightly tapered so that it will fit into the segments and then after the shell is spun the whole assembly, shell, segments, and cover plate can be taken off the arbor. The segments

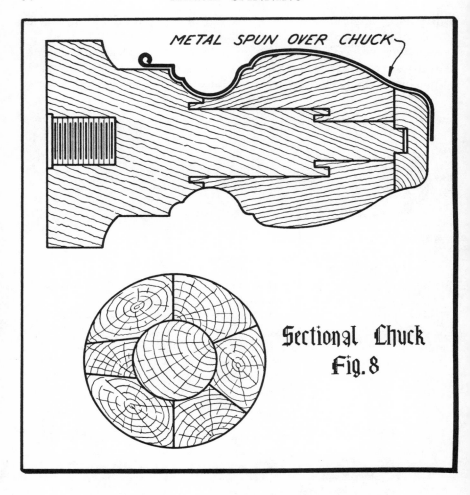

METAL SPUN OVER CHUCK

Sectional Chuck
Fig. 8

are then removed beginning with the key piece and following around until they are all removed, after this the cover plate is removed. Ordinarily they are reassembled over the arbor as they are taken from the shell.

Perhaps the most acceptable method of building up a split or sectional chuck is to plane the segments to the required shape first, then glue them together with a piece of paper between the consecutive faces. This method is shown in Figure 8. After the chuck is turned to shape they are torn apart. It is necessary to be very careful in laying out the job so that it will be possible to get the key segment out, especially when the neck is smaller than the swelled section. Another point to be considered is the cover plate. This must be small enough to be easily removed. If breaking-down chucks are used, it may be possible that the cover plate can be eliminated, as the partly spun shell will hold the segments together.

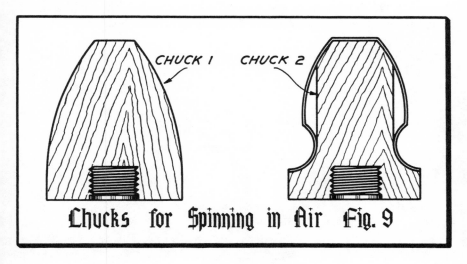

In Figure 9 are shown two chucks over which vaselike projects can be spun. This process is termed spinning in air. It eliminates the making of sectional chucks.

Tail blocks have a flat surface in contact with the work, resin being used when necessary to increase the friction between the tail block and the disk being spun. Whenever an article is being spun which has a

Examples of Sectional Chuck Spinning.

concave or convex base, the tail block is shaped accordingly. The diameter of the tail block should correspond to the size of the base of the article being spun. The tail block may be made of cold-rolled steel for bases of small diameter. In the case of trays, frying pans, or objects with bases of large diameters, the tail block may be made of wood 1½ in. thick, turned to the dimension of the base of the shell to be spun, with a ⅜-in. hole in the center into which the friction unit of the center fits.

Modernized Colonial
Candlestick.

Chapter VI

THE TREATMENT OF THE DIFFERENT METALS

The various metals used in spinning may be divided into three classes: soft, semihard, and hard. The first class offers a minimum resistance to shaping and includes gold, silver, brass, copper, aluminum, zinc, and pewter. In the semihard class, we find monel metal, German silver, and nickel. Steel is placed in the last division. Each of these metals calls for different treatment in forming it to shape.

We will consider copper first as it is very suitable for spinning and is cheap enough so that the beginner can afford to pay for his finished project. It also works up very beautifully and artistically.

In spinning copper the material used should range in thickness from 22 to 26 gauge, depending, of course, on the diameter and depth to which it is to be spun. The No. 26 or lighter gauge is used when the piece to be spun is quite shallow, or when the spinner is more experienced.

Copper should first be annealed before it is placed on the chuck. This makes the metal feel very soft and yielding, but in the process of spinning and the constant contact with the tools it soon becomes hard and springy. When this occurs, the metal must be annealed again. The annealing process must be as brief as possible and the metal must not be left in the fire to soak. The quickest and most common way to anneal copper is to heat the metal to an iridescent color and then plunge it into cold water. This restores the softness and pliability. If the copper should oxidize during the annealing process, a dipping solution of 5 per cent sulphuric acid will restore it to a fine dull pink.

Brass is the next metal to be considered. It must be prepared and worked the same as copper. It is more difficult to spin as it becomes hard and springy from the friction of the tools more rapidly than copper does and has to be annealed more frequently so it can be spun to the chuck. In spinning brass, the lighter gauge of stock, about 22 to 26 Brown and Sharpe gauge, should be used.

As the color of brass does not change much in annealing, it is a good plan to cover it with oil before heating and then allowing the oil to burn off, then immediately plunging it in cold water. When the coating of oil

37

burns off, the temperature is approximately 1000 degrees Fahrenheit, and so lessens the danger of ruining the metal by overheating.

Perhaps one of the most desirable metals for spinning is pewter, or Brittania metal as it sometimes is called. With this metal, the antiques and the more modern pewter pieces which are so popular now in the better stores, may be duplicated very readily. Pewter does not require annealing as it remains soft while being worked, but great care must be taken not to use too great a pressure or the stretching of the metal will put a hole in the piece and spoil the work. It is advisable to use fairly heavy stock, 18 gauge having proved very satisfactory as it can be spun down to any desired shape. It is easy to keep an even thickness, and takes little effort to manipulate.

Modern pewter is a composition of tin, copper, and antimony and takes a beautiful smooth satin finish which does not darken. The pewter of Colonial days contained lead which accounts for the dull, dark appearance of the pewter articles preserved from those days.

Aluminum does not require annealing and is very easy to spin, but this ease might be termed a fault as aluminum responds to the pressure of the tool so readily that often before the inexperienced spinner is aware of the fact, it is beyond the shape desired and in trying to get it to fit to the chuck the metal is so weakened that holes appear in it. Use 16- to 22-gauge metal.

This metal is very light and can be spun to a depth of 20 or even 30 in. so that it is a very desirable material for large work. One fault to be found with aluminum is that in spinning it sweats black and greasy.

Zinc is metal that is valuable principally in commercial spinning. In fact, it is not recommended for schoolwork as it has a crystalline formation and the friction from the spinning tool makes it difficult to spin, especially when an abrupt corner is desired. Great care must be taken when annealing zinc, and it is advisable not to exceed 375 deg. F. before plunging it into cold water. Some craftsmen anneal it by bringing it to 212 deg. F. and place it on the lathe immediately and spin it while hot.

Gold and silver can be spun very readily but their cost makes them prohibitive for the average craftsman. The most artistic spinning is in gold and sterling silver. Sterling silver is very delicate and great care has to be taken not to allow it to become dirty and scratched. If the silver is stretched or thinned in thickness, it becomes so weakened that it is almost impossible to finish the article.

German silver or nickel may also be spun into many shapes. It requires annealing oftener than either copper or brass. It is rather difficult to spin as it is tough and hard. The higher the percentage of nickel in German silver, the harder it is to spin.

Monel metal is a composition of nickel and copper. It is quite difficult to spin as it hardens very rapidly in the spinning process and so requires annealing frequently. It is a very valuable metal in industry as it can be adapted to a large variety of jobs because of its noncorrosive qualities. It must be spun with long sweeping strokes so that the metal will not need to be annealed too often. Annealing weakens this metal.

It is annealed in the same manner as copper or brass. Bronze tools are used in the spinning of this metal.

Steel is more difficult to work than any of the other metals so far considered. While steel is really a material for commercial spinning, it is nevertheless possible for the student to turn out a considerable variety of projects. Steel must be kept well annealed in order to get satisfactory results. Use 24 to 26 gauge. Bronze tools must be used in spinning steel.

There are several metals that have peculiar characteristics when spun. For example, in spinning copper, the edge of the job should be trimmed often as it has a tendency to become ragged, and if allowed to continue will begin to crack. Zinc has the peculiar property of stretching along the grain rather than across it. This excess metal across a diameter at right angles will become a nuisance and must be trimmed often to maintain a uniform edge. All other metals maintain a fairly uniform edge without taking special precaution. The types of articles that can be spun from these various metals will be discussed in a later chapter.

ANNEALING TABLE

	Degrees Fahrenheit	Color, etc.
Monel Metal	1700	Bright yellow
Steel (C.R.S.)	1200	Bright cherry red
Aluminum	650	Will just char white-pine sawdust
Copper	1000	Very dull red, iridescent
Brass	1000	Very dull red when auto oil burns off
Zinc	212–375	Boiling water, spin hot
Pewter	0	No annealing required
Lead	0	No annealing required

Monel metal, copper, and brass should be plunged in cold water immediately after the annealing temperature has been attained. Steel should be permitted to cool slowly.

Aluminum in the gauges spoken of in this chapter seldom requires annealing at all when spun by a skillful spinner. The annealing table gives the temperature in degrees Fahrenheit at which metals should be annealed, and also gives color or other indication when these temperatures have been reached so that the spinners who are in a metal shop not equipped with an annealing furnace with the temperature controlled by a pyrometer may do their annealing satisfactorily.

All of these metals can be given a very high polish by using a fine grade of emery cloth or steel wool. The gloss on copper and brass may be kept by waxing or lacquering the finished articles. Any good white metal polish will serve to keep the other metals bright.

Example of Early American
Spinning.

Chapter VII

LUBRICANTS USED IN METAL SPINNING

Friction between the head of the spinning tool and the disk being spun develops heat. To reduce this heat and to keep the tools from tearing, scratching, and cutting the metal, with consequent damage to the spinning tools, a lubricant must be used on the disk while it is being spun. This lubricant should be applied as often as necessary to prevent the metal from being scratched or cut. Many different kinds of lubricants are used, varying with the kind of metal being spun, the season of the year, the warmth of the shop, and to some degree, the personal preference of the craftsman.

CHART OF LUBRICANTS

The lubricants are listed in reference to the various metals in order of the authors' preference:

Steel	Laundry soap; sheep's tallow.
Aluminum	Sheep's tallow and oil mixture; heavy oil; tallow candle; sheep's tallow.
Monel metal	Sheep's tallow.
Copper	Soap and oil mixture; soft soap; tallow and oil mixture; tallow candle.
Brass	Tallow and oil mixture; tallow candle; soap and oil mixture; soft soap.
Pewter	Soap and oil mixture; tallow candle.
Lead	Tallow candle; tallow and oil mixture.
Zinc	Tallow candle; tallow and oil mixture.
Silver	Tallow candle.
Gold	Tallow candle.

We have found the following mixtures to be very satisfactory and inexpensive.

Tallow and Oil Mixture

The proportion of tallow to oil varies with the season of the year or the temperature of the room. In the hot summer months a very small quantity of engine oil is added to the tallow and both melted together.

One-half pint of oil to 2 pounds of tallow is about the right proportion for this mixture. In the winter months more oil may be added. The point is to have a mixture that will adhere to the disk for a long time.

Soap and Oil Mixture

Shave one cake of yellow laundry soap into fine chips, add 3 pints of water and bring to a boil. Stir until the soap is thoroughly dissolved. Remove from the stove and add from 1 to 1½ quarts of S.A.E. No. 30 engine oil. Beat with a wooden paddle to a creamy mass. Pack into cans for future use. This mixture when cold should be of the consistency of No. 3 cup grease.

A very practical way to apply the lubricant to the spinning disk is to prepare a lubricating roll of cloth, by taking a piece of porous cloth, 12 by 18 in. and thoroughly smear it with the lubricant. Then roll the cloth tightly lengthwise and tie with string. Care must be exercised not

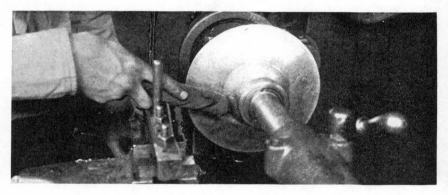

Lubricating the Disk.

to permit the metal to get dry at any time or cutting will result. Beginners usually overdo the applying of lubricants. A small amount applied often, should be the rule.

In the spinning of metals where a tallow candle is used as a lubricant, the candle is applied directly to the revolving disk of metal. Care must be exercised in using this lubricant so that the hand of the spinner will not come in contact with the edge of the metal.

Some spinners lubricate their spinning tools. This is a matter of individual preference, and is not strictly necessary as the lubricant used on the disk will be sufficient to eliminate any excess amount of friction between the tool and the metal.

Chapter VIII

TECHNIQUE OF METAL SPINNING

In order to get an understanding of what metal spinning actually is, one must strive to get a clear conception of how metal behaves during the spinning process. It is easy to understand the behavior of metal while it is being forged, when it is poured at the foundry, when it is rolled into bars or sheets, when it is formed between dies, and when it is shaped by removing some of the metal on the engine lathe. The actual process of spinning metal, however, requires special description, as it is entirely different from any of those mentioned.

Metal spinning is the art of shaping a spinning disk over a wood or metal chuck by compressing it with a blunt-nosed tool. The metal disk under the action of the tool actually contracts in diameter by small degrees and gradually assumes the shape of the chuck. The metal of the disk seems to flow, although it is cold, much as though a sheet of pie dough is formed by the pastry cook into a pie pan.

It would be a more perfect analogy if we assumed that the cook forms the sheet of pie dough over the outside of the pie pan instead of over the inside. The comparison continues also to the method of trimming the ragged edges of metal from the chuck even as the pastry cook trims the ragged edges of dough over the edges of the pie pan. If we grant that the cook used a spinning pie pan upon which he laid the sheet of pie dough and shaped the dough to the outside pan by means of gradual pressure applied with his fingers, we would have a complete resemblance to the metal-spinning process.

It would be easy to see where a steady pressure from the center of the pie pan outwards would cause the dough to thin excessively. The same is true in the metal-spinning process. Also we can see whereby this excessive thinning could be corrected by moving the fingers from the rim of the pan to the center in order to increase the thickness of the pie dough in the pan. The same thing is true in the behavior of metal in metal spinning. It must be understood that this analogy is true only in theory; in actual spinning the metal does not flow so smoothly. The outer edge of the disk as it shrinks in circumference has a tendency to form wrinkles

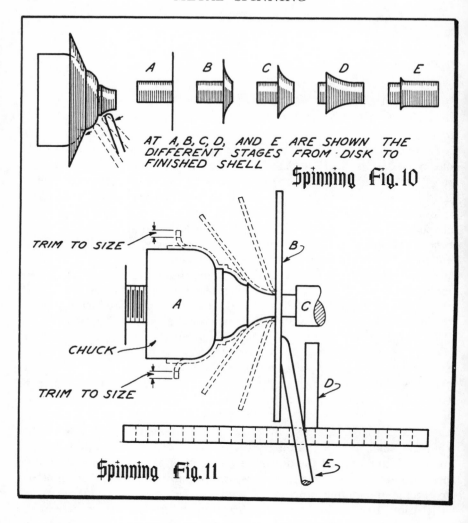

AT A, B, C, D, AND E ARE SHOWN THE DIFFERENT STAGES FROM DISK TO FINISHED SHELL

Spinning Fig. 10

TRIM TO SIZE

CHUCK

TRIM TO SIZE

Spinning Fig. 11

or radial corrugations, and once these wrinkles appear they keep on increasing in size, and unless they are removed they will in time cause the disk to vibrate and, eventually, to develop cracks. The skill of the experienced spinner is shown in keeping these wrinkles at a minimum or by never permitting them to occur.

The experienced spinner will spin a shell from the disk until completely laid down tight to the chuck without the appearance of wrinkles and without noticeable reduction in the thickness of the metal in the finished shell.

Figure 10 illustrates the successive steps in the transformation of the metal disk into a spun shell over a chuck.

A clear understanding of the spinning process may be had by referring to Figure 11, which is a drawing of a simple chuck, disk, and friction block. The disk B is held firmly between the chuck A and the friction unit C by means of pressure applied by the tailstock.

Assume now that A, B, and C are revolving as a unit, at a suitable speed depending on the size of the disk, thickness, and kind of metal being spun. Next, the blunt nose of the spinning tool E is placed against the disk at the point shown in Figure 11, and that pressure is exerted on the fulcrum pin D. This pressure will cause a bend in the metal at the point of application of the spinner's tool. This will cause a contraction of the metal from the outer edge; that is, the outside diameter of the disk begins to decrease.

Next, the point of the spinner's tool is moved under pressure toward the outer edge of the spinning disk. This carries the distortion of the metal out to the edge of the disk and causes the entire disk to assume a conical form. This operation is repeated again and again causing the disk to assume the shape of the form or chuck. This outward movement of the point of the spinner's tool tends to thin the metal of the disk, so in actual practice this process is reversed from time to time, and the point of the spinner's tool is started at the edge of the disk and moved inwards part of the time which tends to cause the metal to retain its thickness.

The amount of pressure applied to the nose of the spinner's tool and the speed with which the tool is moved over the disk will be learned by experience. If the pressure exerted is too great, the disk will wrinkle and start to vibrate. If these vibrations become excessive, breaks will be started at the point where the friction unit touches the disk. Holding the tool too long on one spot also hardens some metals excessively, making annealing necessary before further spinning can be done.

The size of the metal blank necessary to cover a particular chuck may be closely estimated by the experienced spinner. However, through no process of mathematics can the exact diameter be computed. The diameter of the circle of metal necessary to cover a chuck depends upon the design of the form, and no hard and fast rule can be evolved to give the exact diameter. It is well to spin two or three shells from different size blanks and thus determine the diameter of the blank accurately.

This final disk should be sufficiently large to allow some metal being trimmed from the edge before the spinning operation is completed.

It is better to waste a little metal by trimming rather than running the risk of spoiling the chuck and shell by stretching a disk which is too small for the job.

The metal blanks or disks for making the shells may be cut from the metal stock with circular shears. The circular shear may even be provided with a punch for punching out the center hole in the disk, when the shell being spun permits this. Jobs which must have a solid bottom, such as pans, trays, and the like, may be cut on the circular shears, provided a leather or fiber washer is inserted over the central point. The washer should be thick enough to keep the center point of the shear from puncturing the metal disk. The pressure of the leather or fiber washer on the metal should give sufficient friction so that the metal disk may be cut. If the spinner does not have access to a circular shear, the blanks or disks may be cut out with hand snips, and the center holes drilled with a ⅜-in. drill to correspond to the ⅜-in. end of the friction unit where the center hole in the disk is permissible.

Starting the Spinning Process.

The blank or disk is inserted between the chuck which has been firmly screwed on the lathe spindle and the friction unit of the spinner's center. In the case of a disk which has a ⅜-in. hole in it, the ⅜-in. end of the friction unit passes through the hole in the disk and into the recess bored in the chuck.

Next, place enough pressure on the spinning center to firmly hold the disk of metal against the base of the chuck, being careful not to use more pressure than is necessary for firm contact. Resin is sometimes used on the base of the form in order to increase the friction.

In the case of a disk to be used for a job which does not permit the use of a center hole, a tail block of the same size as the base of the finished job must be placed over the ⅜-in. end of the friction unit. The disk is then placed between the tail block and the chuck, centering it carefully, because otherwise the revolving disk may be thrown out when the lathe is started. It must be remembered that it is friction alone, in this type of set-up, which holds the disk in place.

Only sufficient pressure should be used to hold the disk in place and to keep it spinning as a unit with the rest of the spinning assembly. Excessive pressure from the tailstock will cause undue wear on the thrust bearings, spinning center, and the bearings of the lathe spindle.

After the disk is locked in position, it is lubricated with a thin coating of the proper lubricant. The first application of the lubricant is applied to the disk before the lathe is set in motion. Succeeding applications of the lubricant to the spinning disk may be applied very efficiently by the lubricating roll of cloth described in Chapter VII.

The toolrest is placed in position so that the edge of the disk just clears the inside edge of it. The fulcrum pin is located in one of the holes on top of the toolrest, slightly to the right of the edge of the disk. The most satisfactory position can only be learned by experience.

The insertion of disks should always be done by a spinner when the lathe is standing still, and the chuck is at rest. In fact, the rigid observation of this rule will remove the major cause of accidents occurring in metal spinning. Outside of this, the only sources of accident in the entire spinning process are minor ones, such as having the fingers cut on the spinning disk and minor cuts from shavings of metal when the edge is being trimmed.

In industry the experienced spinner who is working on piecework sometimes inserts the disk or blank while the lathe is running. This is exceedingly dangerous, and many commercial shops have a rule that the lathe must be stopped when a new disk is inserted. In some shops, a shield of woven wire is placed behind the metal spinner so that in case of accident no one will be hurt by the flying metal disk but the spinner himself.

After the disk is in place, the lathe must be set in motion at the proper speed. This must take into account the metal being spun, the gauge of the metal, and the size of the disk. It is better to start the spinning at a speed which is too low rather than too high. If the speed is too great for the diameter of the disk, the centrifugal force will make the metal tend to stand at right angles to the chuck. It will then be impossible to make it conform to the shape of the chuck by pressure of the spinning tool. Furthermore, if the pressure of the spinning tool is increased unduly, the wall of the metal will be thinned and the disk will be disrupted and probably injure the spinner.

The handle of the spinner's tool is held under the right arm and close to the body. The spinner should stand slightly to the right of the revolving disk with his feet 8 or 10 in. apart, and his weight bearing mostly on the right foot.

The tongue tool is then placed on top of the spinner's rest to the left of the fulcrum pin and in close contact with the fulcrum pin so as to obtain the necessary leverage in spinning. The point of the tool is brought into contact with the spinning disk at a point somewhat below the horizontal center line of the chuck, and as close to the tail block as possible. Pressure on the spinning disk is now exerted back and forth in a short radius, and as quickly as possible the disk of metal is

Shell at the Cone Stage.

firmly fitted around the base of the form next to the friction unit. Have at least ½ in. of metal tightened onto the form before attempting to shape the remainder of the metal disk to the form. If this is not done, and an effort is made to spin the disk as a whole, the pressure of the spinning tool against the disk of metal toward its outer edge will cause the disk to vibrate and break off around the edge nearest to the friction unit. After the metal has been spun firmly around the first ½ in. of the chuck, the stress and strain comes on a larger area of metal than would otherwise be the case.

The actual work in metal spinning is done by motions of the entire body, since a spinner would tire quickly if he attempted to exert the leverage necessary for a long period of time by means of his arms only. The amount of pressure applied to the disk will be learned quickly. If the pressure is too great, the disk will wrinkle, or it will thin the metal even to the point of rupture. As the blank assumes a conical shape during

Using the Backstick.

the spinning process, the fulcrum pin is moved to another hole on the toolrest, thus giving the tool a better leverage. Instead of working the tool continuously from the center out to the edge of the disk and then repeating this operation, it is well to often reverse the operation and work the point of the tool from the edge toward the center of the revolving disk. This will aid in retaining the thickness of the metal instead of drawing it out thinner. Care should be taken in this operation, however, as the inward movement of the tool may cause the metal to bulge at the point where the blank is held by the chuck and the friction unit. It may even cause it to flow backwards over the friction unit. The movement of the spinner's tool therefore should not be too great, especially in the beginning of the spinning process. A firm contact between the metal disk and the chuck having been obtained at the beginning of the spinning operation, this contact surface is gradually increased due to the pressure of the spinning tool. If the pressure of the tool is excessive, buckling or wrinkling of the disk will ensue. Should this happen, stop the lathe immediately, and remove and anneal the shell. Wrinkling and buckling can usually be prevented by not exerting too much pressure on the spinning tool and by holding the backstick in the operator's left hand on the left side of the disk exactly opposite the point of contact of the spinner's tool and drawing it to the outer edge of the disk as the point of the spinner's tool proceeds to the outer edge, and following back toward the center when the spinner's tool is moved in that direction. If the strokes of the spinner's tool are alternated both inwards and outwards properly, the metal will not decrease in gauge noticeably. In fact, it is possible to increase the gauge of some metals, such as pewter.

Truing Up the Shell with a Diamond Point.

The tongue tool is used to start the spinning operation. The majority of spinners use this shape of tool more in the whole spinning process than any other tool. There has never yet been any shape which excels it.

In case wrinkles begin to appear soon after beginning to spin the disk, the amateur spinner will find it very hard to remove them. The only workable way is to anneal the disk immediately and then proceed with a very gentle pressure of the spinning tool on the disk while the chisel point of the backstick is held at all times directly opposite the point of the spinning tool. In this way the chisel point of the backstick acts as a chuck for the metal while it is being used. It is easier to prevent wrinkles from forming than it is to remove them by skillful spinning.

Before the final edge of the disk is laid down to the chuck, the disk must be cut to size with the diamond-point tool. The proper time for trimming the edge of the disk has arrived when its rim has been laid to within ¼ in. of the chuck. The backstick and spinning tool must then be used to turn the edge of the metal at right angles to the spinning chuck.

Next the toolrest should be moved closer to the edge of the spinning disk and the cutting edge of the diamond point brought in contact with it. Cut the disk down to the proper circumference, exercising great care to produce a smooth, perfect edge. After the edge is trimmed, the flange is laid down to the chuck. In case a bead is to be placed on the shell, the metal is spun to the full length of the chuck before trimming. Then the flange of metal is turned into a bead with the beading tool or backstick and tongue tool. When trimming an edge, there is often a certain amount of chatter. To overcome the chattering, the diamond point may be held so that the metal is pressed slightly to one side. The shape of the diamond point permits the spinner to stand to one side when trimming the edge of the disk so that his head is out of the way of flying chips.

Care should be exercised not to spin a shell too tightly on the chuck or difficulty may be had in its removal. In case the shell apparently is stuck solid to the chuck and cannot be removed, the entire surface of the shell should be gone over lightly with the planishing tool or flat side of the tongue tool. This will enlarge the shell slightly so that it may be removed with ease.

The round-nosed tool is laid aside and one of the other spinner's tools is used whenever the necessity of the work requires it.

In spinning copper the edge of the disk should be trimmed often since copper has a tendency to crack and become ragged at the edge during the spinning process. If the disk is not trimmed shortly after the cracks have appeared, they will quickly become more pronounced. The rule for trimming edges should be to trim whenever the condition of the edge shows it to be necessary.

It is always hard for the beginner to estimate whether a certain job can be spun in one operation. That is, by using only one chuck and that finished to size. If he attempts to spin too deep a shell in one operation, the metal will thin excessively or even break before the upper end of the chuck is reached. By using one or more intermediate or breakdown chucks and annealing between each transfer of the shell to the next chuck, finished shells of much greater depth can be spun than would otherwise be the case.

A very safe rule for students is that a height of one third of the diameter of the finished shell may be spun safely with one operation.

The skilled craftsman, however, may exceed this rule very much. Even

among the students there are some who are able to spin pewter shells
to twice the length of the diameter at one operation. Copper also has
been spun to a height that exceeds the diameter of the shell. No hard-
and-fast rule can be evolved as to the use of intermediate chucks, since
the various factors involved are the gauges and kind of metal used, the
shape of the chuck, and the skill of the operator.

Final Step in Spinning Shell.

Placing a bead on the edge of a shell is done by means of a beading
tool. Care must be taken to see that the flange stands up from the
chuck, enough to form the circumference of the bead. The size of the
flange is in every case a matter of some experiment. When the correct
amount of material has been determined, it is trimmed to that size in
every case. The bead roll is brought into action and the bead is given
a start by holding the tool at a slight angle. The tool is gradually
straightened until the bead is perfectly formed.

Knurling tools may be used to form a decorative effect on the outside
of a shell. Knurls may be bought in a variety of patterns and their use
is very easily acquired. Care should be taken to see that when the knurl
is first brought in contact with the work, it is started properly. It should
rotate with the shell as though they were gears being driven together.
In this way a perfect pattern of the knurl is obtained as it is pressed
into the shell. This can be done only when the knurling wheel is sunk
into the metal of the shell so that it turns without slipping or skipping.
The pressure should be applied to the knurl when the spindle is dead.
Then the chuck should be turned back and forth by hand until the knurl

is forced into the metal sufficiently to prevent slipping. The power may then be turned on and a perfect pattern produced.

It should be noted that tapering shells of light gauge can often be spun successfully two or even three at a time on the preliminary breaking-down chucks. Of course, on the final chuck, only one at a time should be spun.

"Spinning in air" is a term which is often used when the neck of a vaselike shell is spun smaller than the body of the shell. This requires the use of two chucks and the process is clearly shown by referring to Figure 9.

Actual spinning in air, however, is of much broader use in metal spinning. No shell is ever spun without some actual spinning in air taking place while the disk is being laid down to the chuck.

Example of Early American
Spinning.

Chapter IX

PROJECTS

In order to help the students of metal spinning to get a better working knowledge of the craft, the authors are submitting a number of projects.

All of these projects have been made in a school metal shop and have proved to be satisfactory and to comply with popular demands. Only those that the students are capable of making have been selected.

In making these different projects, the spinner progresses from the simple processes in the making of trays, plates, and bowls to the more difficult methods used in the spinning of lamps. These require the fitting of two shells together.

The most complicated and difficult project shown is the vase. This requires the use of sectional or spinning-in-air chucks and demands a high degree of ability.

Group of Vases.

Most of these projects have been made of pewter as it is easily handled in the spinning and makes a very beautiful article. But in the construction of the lamps, copper has proved to be more in demand and works up very artistically.

One of the most popular designs offered is the nut dish. It not only gives skill in spinning but offers an opportunity for the piercing of metal

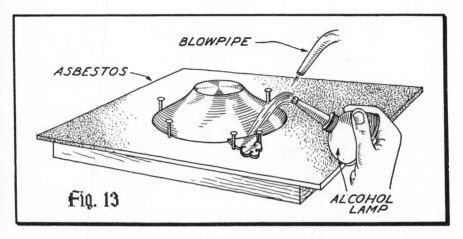

Fig. 13

BLOWPIPE

ASBESTOS

ALCOHOL LAMP

in the making of the handles, and gives practice in soldering when joining the handles to the bowl. These nut dishes are a modernized copy of the Colonial porringer.

The candlesticks and comports are also made in parts, that must be soldered together. This soldering process is shown in Figure 13. The soldering of pewter is quite difficult as the melting point of the metal is nearly the same as the melting point of the solder used.

Projects of Pewter.

First a perfect joint is made between the parts, then a flux is applied (a good flux for soldering pewter is made by adding 10 drops of hydrochloric acid to 1 ounce of glycerin), next small pieces of solder (about 1/16 by 3/16 in.) are laid along the joint about ⅛ in. apart. Heat is applied by means of an alcohol lamp or Bunsen burner and a blowpipe. The flame should be kept moving as the solder follows the heat. Care must be taken not to use too much solder as this results in extra work

Cigarette Box and Trays.

and a careless job. In using a blowpipe the end of it should be kept out of the flame. Before the beginners attempt to solder pewter they should practice with some scrap pieces in order to see just how the solder acts when the heat is applied to it.

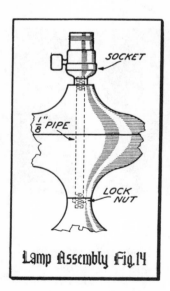

Lamp Assembly Fig.14

Above is the Assembly of the Pewter Lamp Shown at the Right.

The surfaces of the jewel and cigarette boxes may be enriched by soldering a design of copper or brass on them. The copper or brass on the pewter is very effective.

The making of the sugar bowl and cream pitcher involves the use of the sectional chuck. This is necessitated by their shape, as the center portion is larger than the opening at the top.

The beverage set, which consists of a tray and six small tumblers, is very attractive but very simple to make. The spinning of both the tray and the tumblers requires the use of tail blocks. The decoration on the tumbler may be applied either with the diamond-point tool or by using the knurling tool.

In order to eliminate sharp edges on projects like trays, comports, and ash trays, the edge is rolled with a beading tool, tongue tool, or backstick. This also strengthens the article and improves its appearance.

After the shells for a lamp have been spun, the assembling is very simple. A piece of ⅛-in. pipe cut to length and threaded on each end is all that is necessary. A lock nut is used at the bottom and the socket is screwed on the other end of the pipe to hold the three pieces together. This is shown in Figure 14.

After one has learned to spin, he will be able to add innumerable projects to those offered by the authors. It has been their desire to suggest and illustrate projects of accepted and good design, which show practically all the fundamentals of metal spinning.

PROJECTS

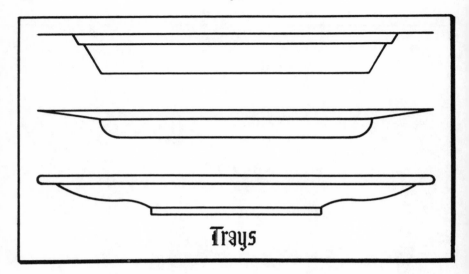

Trays

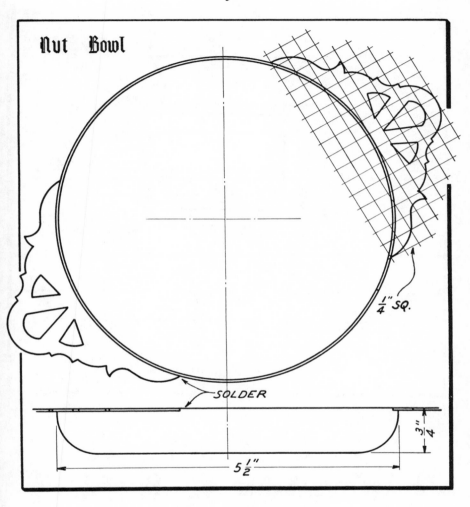

Nut Bowl

$\frac{1}{4}$" SQ.

SOLDER

$\frac{3}{4}$"

$5\frac{1}{2}$"

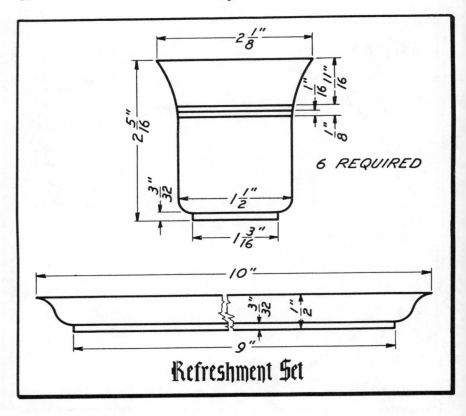

Refreshment Set

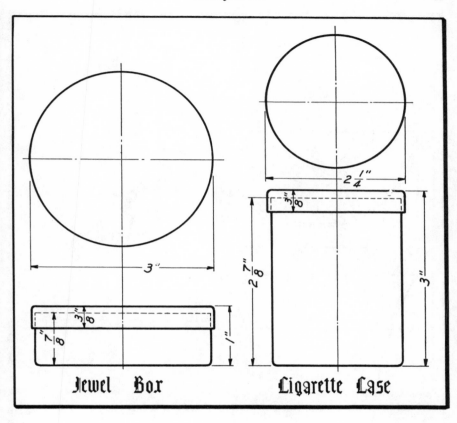

Jewel Box   Cigarette Case

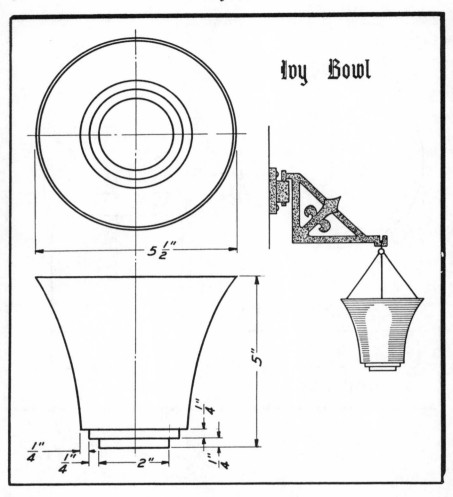

Ivy Bowl

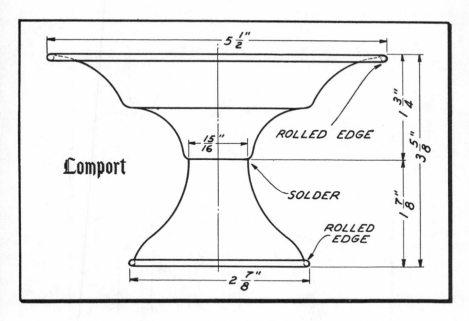

Comport

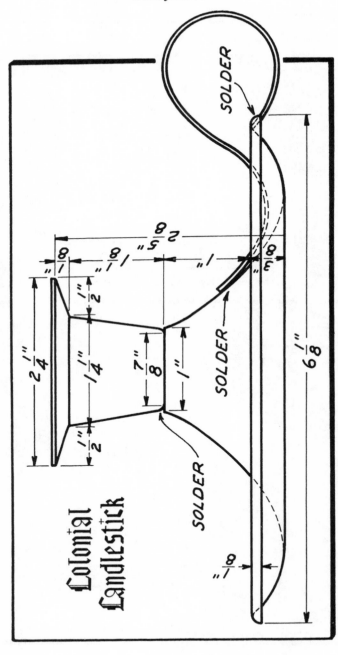

Colonial Candlestick

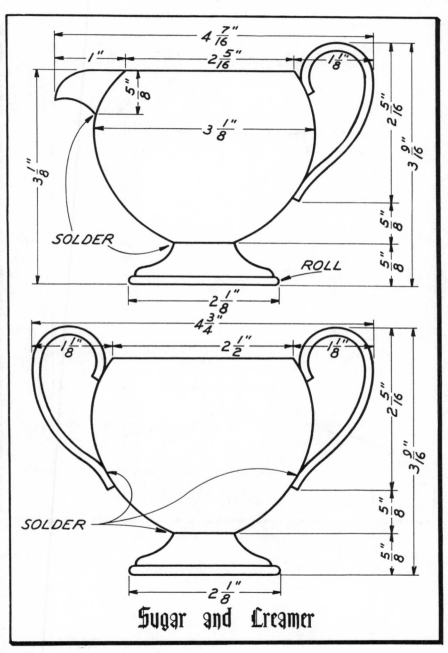

Sugar and Creamer

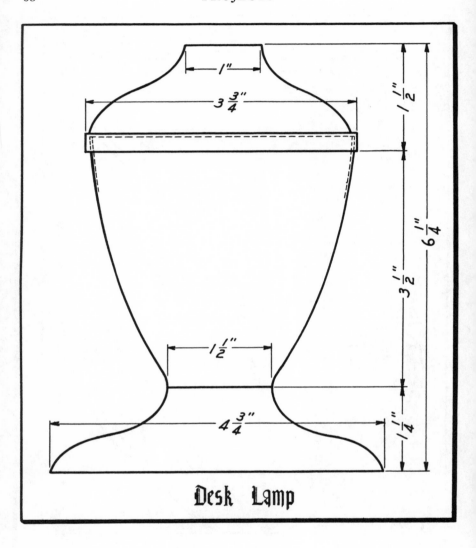

Desk Lamp

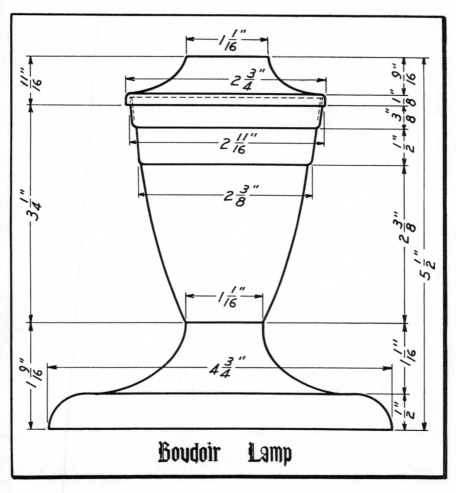

Boudoir Lamp

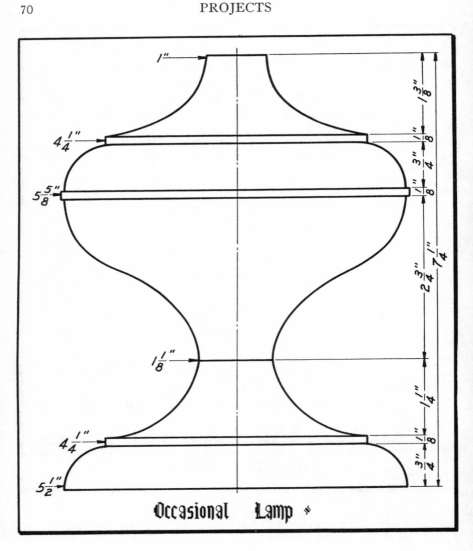

Occasional Lamp

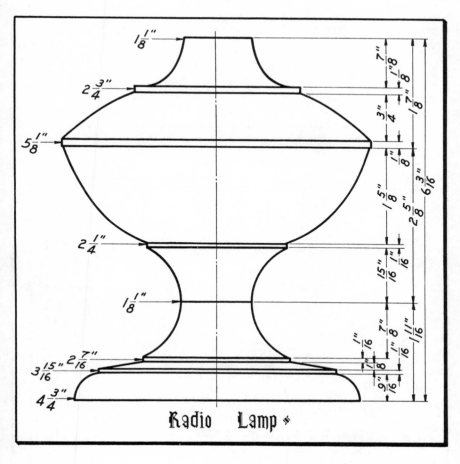

Radio Lamp

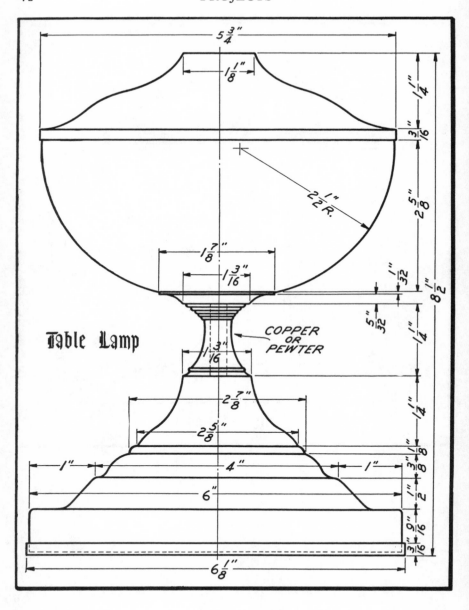

Table Lamp

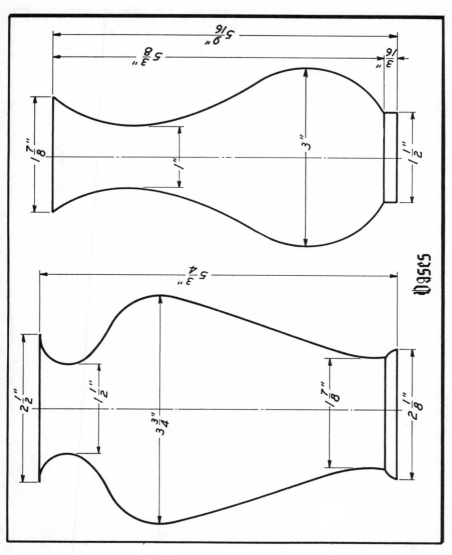

Vases

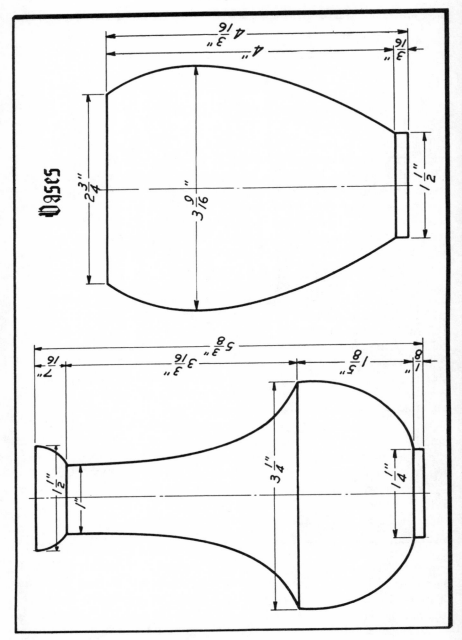

Vases

Chapter X
APPENDIX FOR TEACHERS

This chapter is intended primarily for the teacher of metalwork who is awake to the advantage of adding a new activity to his shop.

In these days of high-speed production, the more versatile students become in school, the more valuable they are going to be in industry.

Metal spinning is a very desirable and valuable unit to add to the school shop as it is one of the few crafts that is not overcrowded in the industrial world. A previous chapter in this book discusses the cause of the scarcity of metal spinners and indicates the new fields that are now open to them.

Equipping the school shop for metal spinning cannot be done without considerable thought, study, and effort. When once installed, however, the metal-spinning equipment will be in operation every period in the day. It is not uncommon that after the school day is over, boys ask to remain to finish up a piece of work.

It has been mentioned that the school shop can be equipped for metal spinning at small expense, but where cost does not have to be considered, regular metal-spinning lathes, spinning centers, and spinning tools may all be bought from reliable manufacturers.

In all branches of industrial arts, safety must be considered. Metal spinning too, has its dangers. When the disk of metal is revolving in the lathe it can be compared to a circular saw. Even though it does not have teeth, yet it is very sharp and can cut a pupil quite badly.

To guard against hazards of this kind, the following "Safety First" rules have been set up:

Never insert a disk when the machine is running.

Always be positive that the tailstock is adjusted so that the friction unit makes a solid contact and that the disk cannot fly off and hit some-one. For this same reason, when spinning projects that require tail blocks, never stand in front of the revolving disk when first starting the lathe. This is also likely to happen if oil and grease are allowed to remain on the tail block.

When lubricating the disk, keep the roll of lubricant away from the edge of the disk so that it will not catch and pull the hand of the spinner against the sharp edge.

Do not stand in line with the revolving disk when using the diamond-point tool as flying chips may cause injury to the eyes. The same danger exists when truing a shell. It is a wise precaution, therefore, to use goggles when doing this kind of work.

If all the foregoing precautions are followed, the dangers in metal spinning are reduced to a minimum.

The teacher of this work will find some difficulty at first in keeping the chucks in shape. Students with little experience will use too much pressure at times on the metal, and this will cut grooves into the chuck. It will then be impossible to remove the shell without tearing the metal. Before such a chuck can then be used again it must be trued up.

Another way of damaging a chuck is by spinning the shell down to the chuck, without removing the burr left on the metal when the edge is trimmed.

The student should be cautioned against punching holes in the disk with the friction unit as the metal punched out is forced into the hole in the chuck, thereby enlarging it. This causes the disk to run out of true.

As most chucks are made of wood, the job of truing them up is not so very difficult.

If cast-iron chucks are used, care must be taken not to get them dented, because then they must be trued up on the lathe. This takes both time and energy.

After metal spinning has been successfully established in the school shop, the public should be acquainted with that fact. An intelligent use of exhibits will help to solve this problem. The first step, perhaps, after arranging such an exhibit, is to send an invitation to the parents, asking them to visit it. They will be quite interested to see what their boy is doing, and how his work compares with that of other boys.

Classroom displays are rather limited in their scope, so corridor displays might be arranged at intervals. These acquaint the whole school with the activities going on in the spinning department and attract the interest and attention of all visitors.

A very good place for an exhibit is in the display room of the school-board headquarters, as this gives teachers and other visitors interested in education an opportunity to see what is being done in the schools.

Perhaps the most ideal place for such a display is in the public library. Many men go to the library who are eager to produce something with their hands and to have a hobby to occupy their leisure. When the men learn how inexpensive it is to do this work, and to equip a shop, many may take up the work in their own workshop at home.

An exhibit of this kind should show not only the finished product but also the various steps in its making. Start with the disk of metal, the chuck, the unfinished shell, the polished shell, and finally show the completed object. Job sheets and blueprints also should be made a part of an exhibit of this kind.

It is well to exhibit only the best projects. Display those that will win approval both in workmanship and design.

Great care should be exercised in arranging a metal-spinning display. Use an artistic background, and remember that a few beautifully made articles, attractively arranged, are very much more effective than a large number crowded together.

If the work of a large group is being exhibited and a large number of projects must necessarily be on display, they should be arranged in groups of similar designs. The more artistic projects should form one group while those of a strictly utilitarian value, like kitchen utensils, should form another.

Neatly lettered cards telling the name of the article and of the student who made it should be a part of every exhibit.

The exhibit is the school's best advertisement and it must be planned with the care it deserves so it will bring favorable comments and secure desirable publicity.

Projects Grouped for Display.

INDEX